I'm In Debt, Over 40, With No Retirement Savings.

HELP!

How to Get Out of Debt and Start Saving for Retirement Now

John L. White

First Edition

Everlove and Bohannon Publishing
Wesley Chapel, FL

I'm In Debt, Over 40, With No Retirement Savings
HELP!
How to Get Out of Debt and Start Saving for Retirement Now
by John L. White

Published by:
Everlove and Bohannon Publishing
Post Office Box 7411
Wesley Chapel, FL 33544-0107
Everlovebohannon@aol.com

ISBN: 0-9740687-4-8
First Printing 2003
Printed in the United States of America

Publisher's Cataloging-in-Publication
(Provided by Quality Books, Inc.)

White, John L., 1957-
    I'm in debt, over 40, with no retirement savings :
    help! : how to get out of debt and start saving for
    retirement now / John L. White. -- 1st ed.
        p.cm.
    Includes bibliographical references and index.
    LCCN 2003092353
    ISBN 0-9740687-4-8

    1. Middle aged persons--Finance, Personal.
2. Consumer credit. 3. Retirement--Planning. I. Title.

HG179.W5228 2003   332.024'0564
                          QBI03-200402

Dedication

This book is dedicated to my parents, Mable and Jimmie White.

Everything I am and have achieved in this life can be attributed to their wise and loving influence.

Acknowledgments

I would like to thank John P. Greaney, Gillette Edmunds, John F. Wasik, and David Chilton for taking the time to review and provide comments on selected chapters of the manuscript.

Many thanks to Michael V. Addessi for taking the time to review the manuscript and provide valuable feedback.

I want to thank my brother, James A. White, Ph.D., Sean Cavanagh, Mike Woss, and Denise Janes for their valuable input on an early draft of the manuscript.

Thanks and all my love to my beautiful wife, Keri, for putting up with my wild ideas and listening to my extremely vocal opinions during our many wonderful years of marriage.

I also want to acknowledge my two beautiful, intelligent daughters, Mary and Kathleen, who have brought so much joy and love into my life.

Contents

Acknowledgments
Disclaimer

Introduction ...9

PART ONE
Getting Your Mind Right

My Situation and How I Got There ...*15*

Put the Past Behind You, the Only Thing That matters is Tomorrow ...*27*

Work: What is it, and Why Do You Do it? ...*29*

Retirement, Will You Get There? ...*33*

What Do You Value? ...*37*

GET OUT OF DEBT ...*39*

Are You a Slave to Your Possessions? A.K.A Stop Buying Junk (This chapter is lovingly dedicated to my wife) ...*43*

The Urge to Collect ...*47*

Do You Know What a Dollar Bill Looks Like These Days? ...*49*

Take the Risk: Talk To Your Spouse or Significant Other ...*51*

PART TWO
Stop The Bleeding

Where Does All the Money Go at the End of the Month? ...*55*

Get Your Expenses Down as Far as You Can ...*59*

Don't Build a New House ...*63*

Don't Buy a Mansion ...*65*

Don't Be Afraid to Buy Your House From the Owner ...*69*

Never Buy a New Car ...*71*

How to Buy a Used Car ...*75*

Should I Buy a Used Car From This Person? ...*81*

Never Buy a Used Car From a Dealer ...*85*

Drive it Till the Wheels Fall Off ...*87*

Why Buy it New, When You Can buy It Used? ...*89*

Car and House Insurance ...*93*

Get Out of the Restaurants and Back in the Kitchen ...*95*

Coupons? Are You Out of Your Mind? ...*97*

Buy In Bulk ...*99*

Teenagers (How to get them out of the house without bankrupting you) ...*101*

Telecommute ...105

Exercise ...107

PART THREE
Saving For Retirement

Just Do It (Join the 401K) ...111

Roth IRA ...113

Don't Give Up Responsibility For Your Money ...115

Build a Cushion ...117

Compound Interest ...119

PART FOUR
Keeping Your Mind Right

Total Denial Could Equal Total Disaster ...123

Think For Yourself ...125

Don't Quit ...127

Appendix (The Shopping Decision Tree)...129

Resources ...131

Index ...136

IMPORTANT- DISCLAIMER

Introduction

When I was 40 years old, I came to the realization that I was in debt and had no retirement savings. It was a frightening thought, one of those wake up at 4:00 AM in a cold sweat feelings. I had a wife, two kids, a mortgage, two cars, two dogs, and a cat to support. I also had no savings. Worse than that, I was in debt, credit card debt. The worst kind of debt there is, about eighteen thousand dollars worth.

Maybe it seems strange that someone could be that old before they fully realized the situation they were in, but it happened to me. What is also strange is logically I knew the position we were in before I was 40, but emotionally, I had managed to avoid facing it. I had pushed my feelings and emotions about it down so deep that I didn't have to face it. I had tried to convince myself that it was OK to live like that, and I guess I had done a pretty good job. But then I hit a wall and could not stop thinking and worrying about it. I had to face the grim reality that I was a middle-aged man with no savings and a substantial burden of debt to carry. That's the bad news. The good news is that I did come to that realization. That was the first step to being able to do something about it. If you want something bad enough or if something bothers you enough to make you uncomfortable, it can spur you to action. I know it did for me.

Since you are reading this, maybe you are at the point where you want to do something about your financial situation too.

After this personal epiphany of sorts, one of the first things I did was to read several books about retirement and investing. I'm an avid reader, so my first inclination for almost any situation is to read about it and study it to death. After reading a few books, I noticed that most of them only spoke to strategies for investing, saving money, and retirement. While that's definitely a piece of the puzzle, what I came to realize is that investment strategies don't mean much if you haven't changed your attitude and perceptions about money and possessions. Even if you manage to claw your way out of the hole of debt you've dug for yourself, if you don't change your mindset, over time, you will end up in the same place you were before because it's your attitude and life choices that got you into the situation you're in. Therefore, the purpose of this book is not only to discuss particular investment and saving strategies, but also attitudes and choices in life that can lead you out of debt and allow you to put some money aside for retirement.

One other note about financial books. A lot of them are just drop dead boring. I hope that by providing real life examples, this book will be a little easier to stick with.

What may be of particular interest to you is this book is not written by a professional financial advisor or money manager. I currently work as a Database Administrator for a large multi-national corporation. I offer you my own experiences and strategies for getting out of debt and staying out of debt. But more importantly, I discuss the changes in my attitude toward debt, money, and to a fair extent, my life, because that's what has to happen if you want to stay out of debt and start developing retirement savings. Like the famous line in the movie Cool Hand Luke, you've "Got to get your mind right".

Everything here is real, there's nothing theoretical. All of the experiences and strategies are things I have done in my own life, and they work. And no, this is not one of those "I'm now worth a half a million dollars, and I did it in five years" books. However, I now have no credit card debt and have a positive net worth (approximately One hundred thousand dollars), and with each passing day, that amount increases.

If you apply the ideas and strategies in this book, your financial situation will also improve. I have no doubt that you will be better off financially than you are today.

PART ONE

Getting Your Mind Right

My Situation and How I Got There

While this is not an autobiography, I think it's worthwhile to give you some background about career and financial decisions that my wife Keri and I have made over the years. It helps to explain how we got into debt. Maybe some of it will sound familiar to you.

When I met Keri, she was eighteen and I was twenty-two. That seems incredibly young to me now, but it didn't back then. Neither of us had college degrees. There was one other thing that neither of us had: debt. That's right, we were both debt free when we met.

She was a waitress and I was a lineman at a power company (I was the guy who turns the lights back on after a thunderstorm). When I met Keri, I did not have a credit card, and as unusual as it sounds, I did not have a checking account. The only account I did have was an old savings account that my parents had opened jointly with me when I was a kid. Maybe you're wondering, how did I pay my bills? I paid them with money orders. Some I even paid in person, with cash.

When I got my paycheck on Friday afternoon, I would drive over to the Savings and Loan to cash it. I would stuff that wad of bills into my left front pocket and walk around feeling like a King. Looking back, that strategy doesn't look so bad now. Everything was on a cash basis. The opportunity to create debt did not exist. If I didn't have it, I couldn't spend it.

When Keri was twenty and I was twenty-four, we got married. Not long after, we had a discussion about our careers and our future desires and wants. She revealed that she wanted to work as a bookkeeper or an accountant. I also told her that somewhere down the road, I knew I had to make a career change. Being a Lineman is something that's fine when you're a young man, but it was not what I wanted to do when I was forty years old. However, at that time, I had no idea what my new career might be.

We decided that she should quit her job so she could go to school and acquire an accounting degree from the local community college. After she began working in her new profession, it would allow me the opportunity to make a career change too. With hindsight, it was one of the best decisions we ever made.

By the time I was twenty-seven, I had gotten to the point where I hated my job with the power company. Well, not necessarily the job itself, but the management. The general manager of the branch office I worked in was a mean spirited individual. He actually said this to Keri and me once: "You know, when a young guy starts working here and he buys a new car, we know we have him for a little while. But then, when he gets married and buys a house, we know we have him for life." That is an amazing statement for someone to make. But once you get past the arrogance of it, you'll find that there's some truth contained within it. In a way, that statement is what this book is all about.

In addition to his impressive verbal skills, he was a "Crack the whip" kind of guy who was bound and determined to inspire fear in his employees. He thought that was how you motivated people. And you know, he was right. Eventually, it motivated me right out the front door. When I left that job, I had no idea or plan for what I would do. I know some of our friends thought I was crazy. Working at the power company was a job you just didn't walk away from. But it had gotten to the point where I couldn't stomach it anymore. I had to leave.

I spent the next two years working different jobs. One of those was working for a foreign-based company that had opened a branch office in Florida. They produced automated equipment for bakeries. My job was assembling and wiring electronic panels that were used to control the automated equipment. The main component of the control panel was a rudimentary computer known as a Programmable Logic Controller.

After I had assembled the control panel, I would wire it up in the warehouse so it could be programmed and tested. The construction of the building I worked in was designed such that the programmer's offices had glass walls that extended into the warehouse. While I was out there assembling the panels, I could look through those glass walls into their air conditioned offices and watch them "working". These were the primary work behaviors I observed: Sitting at a desk reading, sitting at a desk looking at a computer, sitting and talking to other programmers, and sitting and drinking coffee. From all outward appearances, this was obviously a job worthy of further investigation. I got my hands on some of the manuals used to program the controllers and took them home to read.

Fortunately, the company soon experienced a large growth spurt, which taxed the limits of the programming staff. Because they were so busy, there was no one available to program this one little system that was going to be installed in Mexico. I took a shot at it and found out that it wasn't that difficult.

I had also done some reading about "Jobs of the future". At that time, computer programmer was at the top of the list. Even better, published salary survey information I found indicated that it paid well. So, to my mind, this job seemed to be perfect. Top pay, high demand, job description: Read manuals and drink coffee all day. At long last, I had found my life's calling. My dream job awaited...

Now that I had a taste of the good life, I couldn't bear to perform manual labor any longer. I was "beyond that". I decided that it was my turn to attend the community college full time while my wife supported us. I promptly quit my job and enrolled in Data Processing classes. I completed my Associate's degree in a little over one year. Feeling pumped from my success at school, armed with my little two year Data Processing degree, I was a proud thirty-year-old, ready to make the big bucks.

With great expectations, I started applying for programming jobs and waited for the offers to roll in. I waited, and waited, and then I waited some more... four months later, no job offers... Could it possibly be that I was competing against twenty-two year old graduates with Bachelor's degrees from prestigious universities? Or even worse... experienced, out of work programmers, looking for a job? With each passing day, my spirits dropped.

Just when things were really starting to look bleak, our fortunes changed. At that time, my wife was working as a bookkeeper for a home-building partnership. During a discussion with one of the partners, she mentioned that her husband had a degree in Data Processing, but couldn't find a job. As luck would have it, the partner had a friend who managed programmers at a third party insurance administrator. He offered to give her my resume. The interviews went extremely well and I figured they would offer me a job. To say the least, I was excited. I imagined the salary would be good and the benefits would be excellent. Being rather naive about the realities of the corporate world, I had visions of a thirty year career and a nice retirement.

However, when I got the job offer, reality set in: Title: Programmer Trainee, salary: a whopping $16,000 a year. *OUCH !* However, since I had no other prospects, I took the job to get the experience, with the hope that if I worked hard and distinguished myself, I would get promoted and finally get the salary I thought I deserved. As it turns out, I was half right. But before I get to that, there was another life changing event that happened for Keri and me.

Now that I had a job with a large company, we made the biggest decision of our lives. I was past my probationary period and had full medical benefits. Keri and I had now been married for seven years and we wanted to have children. We decided that now was the time.

After our first daughter was born, the plan was for Keri to continue working. Her employer (the same homebuilder), had no problems with her bringing the baby to work every day, and she actually did that for a while until the housing market plummeted. Sadly, the homebuilder went belly up.

At that point, we had to make a decision. One option would have been for us both to continue working and put our child in daycare. But the more we thought about it, neither of us were comfortable with that. We thought it was important for one of us to raise our daughter, not a stranger. We decided that Keri would stay home with the baby. Looking back, there is no doubt that this was the best decision for our family. However, to say that it put us into a difficult financial position is an understatement. What made it even worse was Keri's salary was actually larger than mine was. I believe at the time we made this decision, I was earning the princely sum of a little over $17,000 a year.

I really have to hand it to Keri. During the next few years, she did everything she could to keep our expenses down. She cooked dinner every night and watched every penny we spent. However, in spite of all that, we just couldn't make it on $17,000 a year. Regrettably, we resorted to supplementing the lack of income by using our credit card.

Because of the money crunch we were in, I was eventually forced to change jobs. By that time, I had been promoted to Programmer Analyst, and I had received a couple of raises, but my salary was nowhere near my market value. I learned the unfortunate truth that in many cases, the only way you can really increase your salary is to leave your current employer for another.

I had even gone in and talked to my manager and told him how much I enjoyed working for the company (which was the truth), but that I couldn't pay my bills. He said he would do some research to determine what someone with my skills and experience should be paid and get back with me.

We spoke again in about a week. He said his research revealed that I was right where I should be, that I was making a fair salary for what I was doing. I asked him where he had gotten his information because my sources and research told quite a different story. He was somewhat vague about answering the question. But the bottom line was: no raise for me.

Immediately after, I began a new job search. In a matter of weeks, I received a job offer for about $6,000 more than I was currently making, plus an annual bonus. I wrote up a letter of resignation and presented it to the same manager. He looked at it, then asked if I would mind telling him how much the offer was for. When I told him, he asked me if I would stay if the company matched the offer. At that point, I was thinking to myself: "What? Why didn't he just offer me the money before? Why did I have to go out and get another job offer before they would cough up the money I was worth? "

Fortunately, I was prepared to answer the question because I had done some reading that advised never to accept a counter offer from your company. From that point forward, the company might think you were disloyal, and if there were layoffs, your name could be first on the list. So I thanked him, but then explained I had already accepted the job offer and that I did not like to go back on my word. He was probably thinking to himself: "What a trite notion".

When I started my new job, I found that things were not quite what I had expected. The exciting new project I had been promised when I was interviewed failed to materialize. I was assigned to doing routine programming tasks with virtually no chance of expanding my skills. During a "one on one" interview with the Director (He was the type of upper manager who holds personal meetings with his employees at least once a year), he asked me if I liked what I was doing. I told him no. He asked me if it was challenging. I said no. At the end of the session, he promised me that he would try to find something more interesting and asked me to hang in a little while longer.

He was good for his word. About a month later, he asked if I wanted to interview with the company Database Administrator. He needed a part-time assistant because he had so much work on his plate. I was offered the position and shortly thereafter became a full-time Database Administrator. After about two years of experience in the position, I found myself in a familiar situation: I was making less money than my market value. I had to leave when I was offered a job making $14,000 more than my salary.

I continued to work as a Database Administrator at various companies through the 1990's. During the Dot.com bubble of the late 90's , I was offered a job with a start up company. The same Database Administrator I had worked with previously offered me the job. He had left the company not too long after I had, and was now a Manager at the start up.

The salary offer was extremely attractive with a potential 20 percent bonus and about 7,000 shares of stock (they were soon going public with an IPO). I had never thought I would be in a position to make that kind of money. However, knowing that nothing in this world comes for free, I decided to gather as much information as I could before accepting the offer.

I started inquiring about what the job would demand of me. The deal was I would travel to client sites three days a week and telecommute two days a week. However, I had the gut feeling that when a client is paying a huge hourly rate for a consultant, they want to see his face. During the course of our discussions, I got the distinct impression that I would probably be spending more like five days a week with clients, leaving only two days with my family.

That was the deal breaker for me. If I accepted the job, I would need to stay at least three to four years because there was a four year vesting period for the stock, twenty five percent each year. The more I thought about it, I realized I did not want to miss out on three or four years of my children's lives. No amount of money in the world could bring back those years. I thanked him, but declined the offer.

That company went public shortly after I declined the job offer. During the first year, the stock rose to over eighty dollars a share. I have to admit, it was tough visualizing the amount of money I might have made, but I never regretted the decision. Then the dot com bubble burst and their fortunes changed, along with many other companies. As of this writing, the stock price is now under a dollar a share.

During the time I received that job offer, I was working for a large telecommunications company. The funny thing is, I had never applied for a job with them.

I had originally accepted a position with the company I am currently employed by and had accrued a little over three years of service when they unexpectedly sold the division I worked in to a large telecommunications company.

Eleven months later, I came to work one day and was laid off at five o'clock in the afternoon. Three weeks later, I hired back on again with the old company (the one who had sold me and the one I still work for). Talk about back to the future… What's even more ironic is that I still reported to work at the same place because both companies had employees in the same building.

Fortunately, the dark cloud of getting laid off had a silver lining. I received two months severance pay, which we were able to use to pay off the loan on our Toyota 4 Runner. Also, since I was re hired by the same company I had worked at before, they honored my three plus years of previous employment, so I was not quite two years from my five year pension vestment period. An even more important part of that silver lining is the timing of my layoff. If it had happened after the dot com bubble burst, my job hunting search could have taken much longer with potentially disastrous results for our financial situation.

Another good thing that resulted from my getting laid off was the reinforcement of the importance of getting out of debt and building some retirement savings. I had already experienced my revelation regarding our financial situation and had started taking some steps in the right direction, but getting laid off was just one more thing that drilled the message into my brain like a sledgehammer.

During the past two years, I have seen many of my friends in the high tech field lose their jobs. For every one of them, the job search takes much longer than it used to. Some of them have had to accept jobs making less money. Some have had to move out of state to find work. Some are still looking...

I think the government is attempting to spin control the situation by trying to convince people that our economy is not as bad off as it is actually is. Personally, this is the worst job market I have ever seen. Moreover, in my opinion, we are potentially facing several years of an extremely stagnant job market.

Within the high tech industry, many of the jobs that would normally be filled by Americans are now performed overseas. By now, you have no doubt heard the term "Global Economy". What the Global Economy means to the average American worker is some person overseas will do your job at a fraction of the cost. Make no mistake about it, this is a trend that won't reverse, in fact, it is gaining momentum. Accordingly, I believe the Data Processing job market in America will never be the same again.

To me, these recent events are a clarion call. The time to act is now. The time to get out of debt is now. The time to save for retirement is now.

Put the Past Behind You, the Only Thing that Matters is Tomorrow

Along with the realization of being forty years old and in debt, I started having all of these "What if?" kinds of thoughts. Thoughts like "If I had only saved 10 percent annually since I had started working, I would be so much better off than I am now" or "It's too late now, I'll never save enough money for retirement at this age". To add fuel to the fire, just about every financial book I have read has charts that show how many dollars you will have at age sixty five if you have saved ten percent annually beginning at age twenty five. They assume you've been saving for your entire working life. Man, that's like rubbing salt in the wound.

I suppose quite a few people are fortunate enough to have had the foresight and the discipline to start saving for retirement beginning with their very first job, so by the time they are forty years old, they are sitting on a nice little nest egg. Well, I wasn't one of them. And for a little while, I was kicking myself for not having that foresight or the discipline to have saved on a regular basis.

However, pretty quickly I got to the point where I realized that those kinds of thoughts are a form of evasion. The past is over, never to return. What's the point of beating yourself up about it? Can you go back and change it? So, what's the point of playing those mind games? You will only be torturing yourself.

Perhaps subconsciously, it's a way to deflect attention from what you need to do today, right now, to make things better. The only thing that can be gained from the past is to apply the lessons you have learned from mistakes you have made, and modify your behavior going forward. In this case, what was the mistake? You either didn't save any money for retirement or you didn't save enough money for retirement. So, start saving 10 percent of your salary, or increase the amount you are saving to the amount you want, and then let it go. Don't torture yourself about the past. It does you no good.

If you feel like it's pointless to start saving now because you'll never catch up to where you should be or could have been, look at it this way. If you don't start now, you won't have anything, not a dime. And while you might not have $750,000 or whatever magic dollar figure you would optimally like to have when you retire, you might have $250,000 or $350,000. In my book, that beats the heck out of having nothing.

Work: What is it and Why Do You Do it?

If you have a paying job that you love, consider yourself lucky. Or maybe it's not luck, perhaps you had the personal insight that guided you to a lucrative career that you also happen to love. In that case, by all means, keep doing what you're doing. Unfortunately, there are tons of folks, myself included, who are not in love with their jobs.

My job is just a job to me at this point. It gives me a way to make money so I can put food on the table for my family. I don't hate it, but it doesn't exactly get me juiced either. I have a professional attitude and I do my job well, but there are a hundred other things I would prefer to do with my time, a hundred other interests that I would like to pursue.

Accordingly, there is a major tradeoff involved when I choose to work at a job for the sole purpose of earning a dollar. The tradeoff I am making is this: I am *selling my time for money*. And since my life consists of time, in essence what I am doing is *selling my life for money*. At first, that concept may seem a little extreme or overstated, but, when you really get down to it, that's the deal. Once I fully realized and internalized this, I decided I didn't want to spend one minute that I didn't have to making that tradeoff. But here's the rub: I have a family to support. I have two kids to raise. I can't just chuck it all and run away to Tibet for six months. However, the realization that I am selling my life for money provided me with the drive to retire as soon as I can. To facilitate that, I needed to get out of debt and set aside as much money as I could.

So I made some deals with myself. The first of which was I would continue to work in my job as long as I could. But, I would pursue other interests (like writing a book) outside of my work. I wouldn't wait until I retired to do all those things I had "always wanted to do". Putting your life on hold until you reach some arbitrary level of monetary security doesn't make much sense. It would actually be kind of stupid. I think you need to live your life today and everyday as much as you can.

The second deal I made with myself is if it ever gets to the point where I hate my job and absolutely can't take it anymore, I will leave and either look for a better situation in the same profession, or if need be, seek a different profession. Part of my preference to stay in data processing is based on the logic that if I have to work, I might as well make a decent buck doing it, thereby allowing me to put more money aside.

The third deal I made was I would not work one day past 62 (the minimum age I can collect reduced social security benefits) that I did not want to. Whatever financial situation we were in, either $50,000 or $500,000 in retirement savings, that would be it. If I did not want to work anymore, I was going to hang it up and walk away. Of course, I would like to be able to retire before 62, but 62 is the most conservative estimate.

There is a third group of people who work. They are also working for the money, but they hate their jobs. Every day is a battle to drag themselves into work. They may actually have to deal with physical illness caused by their jobs. If you ever find yourself in that situation, the only advice I can give you is this: you have to find a way out. I don't think anything in this world is worth self-destruction. If you tell yourself you are doing it for your family, you're only kidding yourself. What good are you going to be to them if you have a nervous breakdown or develop some type of stress related illness caused by your job? Worse yet, what if the stress causes you to have a stroke or heart attack? You won't be much use to your family if you're lying six feet under. I don't think my kids would look back and say, "Good old Dad was a great guy. He worked himself to death for us and we really appreciate that."

In this life, each of us has only so much time allotted to us. The exact time each of us has is unknown, but there is no question that the amount is limited. So, what are you going to do? Will you squander all your money away and never be able to retire or will you set something aside so in the future you can devote your time to doing the things you want instead of having to continue to sell your time for a dollar?

Retirement, Will you get There?

At one time it seemed to me like retirement was an eternity away. A distant place that I might get to some day, but it was so remote, I couldn't even focus on it. I had thoughts like: "Hey, I might not even make it to retirement, I could die before then, so I need to live it up today". But when I turned 40, that all changed. I remember thinking: "Hey, just a little while ago, I was 20 years old, in another 20, I'll be 60." All of a sudden, retirement age didn't seem that far away...

Make no mistake, chances are you will see retirement age. That's what they mean when they say the average life span is now 70 plus years of age. Moreover, with new advances in the medical profession, the average life span keeps increasing. Once you reconcile yourself to the idea that you will probably make it to retirement age, the question then becomes: What kind of retirement will you have? I don't know about you, but I'd like to have enough money to travel and live a fairly comfortable lifestyle.

However, the nice company pensions our parents enjoyed are rapidly becoming a thing of the past for most Americans. My employer, along with many other companies converted to what is known as a cash balance pension plan a few years ago. In a Cash Balance Pension, the company sets aside a certain percentage of your salary every month. For me, the amount is five percent of my salary. When I leave the company, I will receive the money in a lump sum. That's it, a done deal. The publicly stated reason for companies converting to a Cash Balance Plan is that it fits today's mobile work force and will benefit employees who change jobs periodically. In my opinion, the real reason is quite different. A cash balance plan will cost a company less money than a traditional pension plan. Accordingly, the average employee will receive less money than with a traditional pension.

I actually consider myself fortunate to still have some form of retirement plan. Many companies now offer no retirement at all. Pretty soon, government jobs may be the only ones that offer pensions. So, if you work for the Government, you might want to consider sticking it out so you can get that pension.

What does all this mean? For me personally, it means my sources of retirement income are social security, whatever money is in my cash balance pension account, and personal savings (401K and Roth IRA).

Contrary to what the doom and gloomers say, social security will not disappear. However, there is a real chance that the benefit amounts will be reduced. The simple fact is there will not be as many workers supporting the retired segment of the population as there are today. The most obvious answers to this looming problem are either to reduce the amount of benefit each person receives or to increase the age at which each person begins to draw benefits.

Have you ever looked at the social security statement the government sends you? Do you think that's going to be enough money to support a comfortable retirement? If like me, you are on a cash balance pension, or maybe no pension at all, where is all the rest of the money going to come from?

When all these factors are taken into consideration, the importance of personal savings becomes paramount. So in answer to the question of: "What kind of retirement will you have?" The answer is simple: It all depends on how much money you managed to save.

What do you Value?

Do you know what your priorities are? Have you ever consciously stopped and thought about them or actually listed them on a piece of paper? Do you value your wife or husband? Do you value your children? Do you value your parents? Do you value yourself? Do you value your time?

I know when I make my list, there are no material things that show up at the top. The real priorities are my family, my time, and my health. None of these things have a monetary value attached to them. You can't buy them.

The only possessions we have that are important to me are ones with sentimental value. The step-stools my father made for our children, old photographs, a bible that my mother bought for my father, my grandfather's watch. But they only mean something to me because they represent someone I value, someone I love. Everything else is just stuff that has the potential to distract my time and energy from what is really important in this life.

No "thing" in this world is now more important to me than having the option to use my time as I see fit. Quite to the contrary, each new "thing" we purchase that we didn't need represents a little piece of my time that I had to forfeit for it. Once I reached these realizations, reducing our debt and saving money wasn't hard at all for me. It has become a way of life.

GET OUT OF DEBT

I cannot over stress the importance of getting out of debt. When you get into debt, you have *mortgaged your future*, plain and simple. You have assumed an obligation to trade your future time (your life) to pay the debt. Not only that, but you have agreed to pay a surplus (the interest) for the use of borrowing the money. Talk about making a deal with the Devil...

If you take on enough debt, you can get to the point where the only thing you are paying is the interest on your debts, you aren't actually paying down the principle. If you ever reach that point, unless you make some changes, you have enslaved yourself to years and years of debt. Pretty sobering thought, eh?

The first thing you have to do is stop accumulating new debt. Every time you reach for that credit card, you need to stop and ask yourself if the thing you want is worth selling your life for. If you think about it that way, it makes it a little harder to whip out that credit card for an impulse buy.

The next thing you need to do is create a strategy to reduce the existing debt you have. I think the best way to approach this is to focus on debts that are non-tax deductible with the highest interest rate. In many cases that might be store credit cards.

If you have enough equity in your home, you can take out a home equity loan or home equity line of credit. That can be used to pay off the existing debts you have. You could very easily reduce your minimum monthly payment and also receive a lower interest rate. The other potential bonus is that it could be tax deductible (you need to confirm this with your accountant). However, what you have to promise yourself and follow through on is this: You have to keep paying the same amount you paid before. Just because you reduced your monthly payment doesn't mean that's all you should pay now. If you keep paying the same amount as before, then you will start reducing the balance.

Another strategy to reduce your debt is to use any monetary windfalls such as bonuses and money you receive as gifts. Instead of blowing it on something, use it to pay down your debts. As I mentioned before, I took the severance money from when I was laid off and used it to pay off the loan on my Toyota 4 runner.

If you have no home equity or impending cash windfalls, you will have to do it the old fashioned way. You will have to reduce the amount of money you spend each month. This book is full of ideas for reducing expenditures. Once you put some of them in place, then you should have extra money to apply to your debts each month.

What helped me through the process of debt reduction was to visualize how good it would feel to finally be rid of that debt, to have a clean slate. I thought about all the possibilities and the freedom I would have when I knew that my future wasn't mortgaged away for some *thing* I once thought was important.

Are You a Slave to Your Possessions? A.K.A. Stop Buying Junk

(This chapter is lovingly dedicated to my wife)

At one point in the past few years, I actually said to Keri during a heated discussion: "I refuse to be a slave to my possessions". Once you have finished laughing yourself silly, let me try to explain what I mean by that statement.

Have you ever noticed how much junk there is in your life? I am purposely using the word junk to make a point, because when I look around my house, many of the things in it, when you get down to it, are really...junk. Even the things that aren't junk now are on their way to becoming junk someday. For example, we have a Maytag washer and dryer. I'll go out on a limb and state that in 25 years or less, they will be classified as junk. When I look in our closets at all the clothes we have, what will most of them be in 10 years? Junk. The next time you go into Goodwill or Salvation

Army, remember that all that junk in there is something that someone bought brand new with their hard earned money.

So, take a look around your house sometime. Do you see any junk? Any shirts, shoes, or pants that you paid good money for and wore only a few times? What about all that junk out in the garage? Is there anything that's broken, that you don't use any more, and you now realize you never really needed? Is there anything out there that was never used at all? I know when I scan our garage, all I see is junk. Junk that I spent my precious time earning money to pay for.

And speaking of time, how much do you spend moving your junk? Cleaning your junk? Do you buy shelves or special containers to store your junk? And worst of all, do you rent a storage building to house your junk? Step back for a moment and think about the wisdom of that decision. You shell out money every month in order to house your junk that you neither use nor see. Not only that, but you paid money for that junk when you bought it. Did you pay cash for it or credit? If you paid credit, are you still paying interest for the junk you don't use in addition to the money for the storage unit every month? If you had taken all the money you spent on the junk, the interest on the purchase of the junk, and the money you spent for the storage unit and saved it instead, how much money would you have today? Would you be any closer to retirement?

Once you understand and internalize the fact that the junk you buy puts you farther away from retirement, I think you are on well on your way to getting control of your finances.

So, what percentage of the junk you buy is something you really need? When you are in the checkout line at the grocery store, before you grab that magazine and plop it down on the conveyor belt with the groceries, stop and think: "Do I really need this?" When you're walking down the aisle at KrapMart (you know which store I'm talking about) and you see that cute little knick knack sitting there, just waiting for you to grab it, ask yourself this: "How important is this thing to my life?" Then ask yourself if it's worth the real price you'll pay for it.

As an aid and a guide to help you during those moments of shopping weakness, I have created a "Shopping Decision Tree" and included it in the appendix. This highly scientific visual aid will help reinforce the "only buy what you really need" attitude that will keep you from purchasing junk that drains your bank account and keeps you one step farther away from retirement.

The Urge to Collect

The previous chapter notwithstanding, I think that humans must be born with an urge to collect. I'm afraid I have a bit of the urge myself. When I was a kid, the thing I collected was comic books. At one time I had over 2,000 of them. I stored them on this massive shelf that occupied one entire wall of my bedroom. I kept the "special" ones in protective plastic bags. I had them categorized and stacked in neat little piles. It gave me a great feeling just to look at them, knowing they were mine.

Adults collect things too. Barbie dolls, Beanie Babies, Longaberger Baskets, Coca Cola items, the list goes on and on...

I think many people rationalize their collecting behavior by thinking it's an "investment". Something along the lines of: "These Barbie dolls are worth a fortune, I could sell them and be sitting on a nice little pile of money". But, how many people actually sell the things they collect? And of the ones who actually sell, how many made money off the transaction? My guess would be not many. If you collect something, at least try to be honest with yourself. What do you really think the chances are that you will cash out some day? If the answer is probably zero, then what you are doing is not investing, it's feeding a habit. Maybe this realization will help you stop or maybe reduce the amount of things you collect.

Keri's weakness is tablecloths. She must have more than fifty of them. We have an entire shelf in our laundry room devoted to tablecloths. Just the other day, she brought home two more. Thankfully, she either purchases them used or buys inexpensive ones.

My weakness is books. I rationalize this behavior to myself because I constantly refer back to them. I reread sections of them periodically. Did you notice I used the word rationalize? Because, can I really justify the expense of the books? Could I live without them? Well... Yeah. But, I like my books.... So what I'm trying to do is reduce the amount of money I spend on them. I have almost totally quit buying books new (You notice I said "almost"). I purchase many of them on the Internet via abebooks.com or half.com.

The message here is if you find it too difficult to quit collecting something or you just don't want to stop collecting, find a way to cut down on the cost of collecting.

I have to confess, there's one other thing I collect now. It's money. I can't explain to you what a warm, fuzzy feeling I get when I look at my 401K balance and watch it increase every month.

Do You Know What a Dollar Bill Looks Like These Days?

Have you discovered that you hardly ever touch real money anymore? Your paycheck is automatically deposited into your checking account. Money to pay your bills is automatically withdrawn from your account. You go out to dinner and you pay with the credit card. You go to the grocery store and whip out the checkbook. Where did all the real money go?

Start using real money again. You know, that green stuff with the goofy oversized pictures of the DWG's (Dead White Guys) on it? Oh, you didn't know they did that? It's been that long since you've seen a twenty?

When you use a credit card, it's too easy to fool yourself into believing it's not as real as real money. However, when you pull those dollars out of your pocket, count them out and have to lay them down, it just seems a little harder to do. In addition, you will be witness to the depletion of your money.

For example: you withdraw $100 from your checking account on Monday, then along comes Thursday and all you have left in your pocket is $5. Where did all of it go? At least you have that feeling of loss. With a credit card, you don't get that kind of feedback. You just sign a piece of paper and away you go, without another thought.

There's another more obvious benefit to using cash. If you don't have it, you don't spend it.

Take the Risk: Talk to Your Spouse or Significant Other

If I told you that my change of attitude concerning money, possessions, and retirement did not cause any friction between Keri and me, that would be a flat out lie.

For many years, I was fairly uninvolved in our personal finances. Keri paid all the bills, did all the grocery shopping, she handled everything. Then, within a relatively short period of time, I started paying the bills, doing grocery shopping, using coupons, etc.

In some cases, I acted like I had invented the wheel. When I started using coupons, I was all fired up about it. I had forgotten that years ago, Keri used to coupon, and I had acted like it was no big deal. So, she had every right to be a little perturbed about my "new attitude".

Another major mistake I have made is questioning Keri on purchases she makes. We finally had a big blow up about it. Now I do my best to try not to question her about the things she buys.

Another area that has been an issue for us is the definition of want and need. Keri's definition is this: "If I want it, I need it". However, my definition is somewhat different. And, in general, there's not much I want or need.

I guess what it comes down to is that we don't always have the same ideas about money and purchases, and in many cases, the best thing to do is just give the other person the space they need to make their own decisions.

If you and your significant other have differences of opinion on money matters, the only advice I can offer is to sit and calmly discuss your thoughts and ideas and try to focus on the goals that you have in common. I know I have the tendency to become obsessed about new ideas and ventures. It helps to try and keep it all in perspective. Don't expect things to change overnight.

PART TWO

Stop The Bleeding

Where Does All The Money Go At The End Of The Month?

It seems that sometimes we are good at making money, but we aren't always good at knowing where it all went at the end of the month. You've probably heard the old saying that you will spend whatever you make. To a large extent, that is true, especially if you aren't aware of where all your money is going.

But you know what? I hate budgets, I really do. I absolutely refuse to do them. So, how do you figure out where all the money is going?

For one month, you can record everything you spent money on. Record even the small purchases. That candy bar you buy from the snack machine at work in the afternoon, write it down. The video you rent on the weekend, write it down. The fee you pay for returning the video a day late, write it down. At the end of the month, run calculations using the frequency of how often you purchased an item to determine how much it will cost you over one year.

Here's an example: 5 candy bars a week at $1 each equals $5 a week. $5 times 50 weeks (deduct 2 weeks for vacation time, when you aren't buying candy from the machine at work) equals $250 a year.

My family averages $8 every week renting videos and probably $8 a month in late fees on them. $8 times 52 weeks equals $416 a year. $8.00 times 12 months (for the late fees) equals $96 a year. $416 plus $96 equals $512 a year just to rent videos! By the way, we are working on eliminating those late fees…

In addition to these everyday expenses, track your monthly expenses. Make sure you include the following:

Monthly Expenses

Mortgage or Rent
Electric
Telephone
Cell Phone
Garbage
Car Payment
Car Insurance
Cable TV
Water
Gas
Tuition (If your kids go to private school)
Lessons (Dance, music, etc.)
Memberships (Gym, Clubs, etc.)
Donations (Church, etc.)
Online Service Provider

Pest control
Clothes
Groceries
Health Insurance
Monthly Medicines
Gifts
Eating out
Entertainment
Car Repair

Annual Expenses

Life Insurance
Real estate Taxes

The purpose of this exercise is to reveal to you where your money is actually spent. You may be surprised at how much the little expenses add up. Once you have this information compiled, you can identify areas where you can reduce your spending.

Get Your Expenses Down as Far as You Can

Getting your expenses down accomplishes several things. Of course it lets you save more money for retirement. It also gives you some freedom in terms of job choices. If you make $60,000 a year and spend all $60,000, it limits your job choices quite a bit. However, if you make $60,000 and only spend $40,000, it gives you a much broader selection of jobs to choose from.

My personal goal is to reduce our fixed monthly expenses as much as possible. When I first started looking at reducing our expenses, the two largest areas were our house payment and truck payment. We recently refinanced the house at 6 1/8 percent. The payment is now $644, a reduction of almost $100 a month. At the writing of this book, interest rates are the lowest they have been in 40 years. If you haven't refinanced your house, it makes a truckload of sense to take advantage of these historically low rates.

The truck payment we had was $360 a month (don't ask me what we were thinking at the time we bought it). We sold the truck for about $100 more than we owed on it and purchased a used conversion van. Our payment on the van is $80 dollars a month. I cannot over stress the importance of that decision. Nothing concerning the quality of our lives has changed and we eliminated $280 of expense every month.

We have no Cable or satellite TV. I can hear you now: "No cable TV? Now that's going just a little too far". We had cable TV about ten years ago, something like 47 channels, and still nothing to watch. The truth is, cable TV is not even available where we live, however, satellite is. But for us, the decision is not just monetary. With two kids in the house, considering some of the things on cable, it's just as well that we don't have it. Also, if not having cable makes you watch less TV and find something else to do, like reading a book or playing with your kids, what's so bad about that? The truth is, we don't miss it at all.

Electricity is another area where you can reduce your monthly bills. Wait a little longer before you turn on the air conditioning in the summer, try to stretch that time between winter and summer when you don't have to heat your home, or cool it. You can also turn the thermostat up a couple of degrees in the summer. If you don't have ceiling fans, install them, they are money savers.

If you don't have a hot water heater timer, install one. If you have one, consider purchasing a second set of switches for it, so it will turn itself on and off twice a day, automatically (this was Keri's idea, and a darn good one). If your water heaters have a little age on them, you might want to replace the elements. When the elements get old, they corrode and are not as energy efficient.

Replace your light bulbs with Compact Fluorescent bulbs. The initial cost is more, but over time, they will cost less to operate and you won't have to change them out as often.

Don't renew your magazine subscriptions. Use the library instead. Also, do you really need to get the paper every day? We used to have a daily subscription, but I can't tell you how many times the paper never came out of the plastic bag. Now we only get the paper on Sunday.

Remember that the main goal here is to reduce or eliminate the regular, recurring bills that you have. And ask yourself: "Do I really need this? Will the quality of my life really be reduced if I don't have cable TV or 5 magazine subscriptions?"

Don't Build a New House

I think you're better off buying an existing house instead of building a new one. Once you get past the emotional issues of wanting a "new" house, you will find there are some compelling reasons why you should not build.

It is generally cheaper to buy an existing house than a new one. When you build a new one, you are paying current construction costs. Also, when you buy a house in an established neighborhood, you know what you're getting.

When you start your house search, you need to consider several factors. You may have heard the saying that the three most important things when buying a house are "Location, Location, and Location". That's one of those sayings that happen to be true. If you buy a nice house in a bad neighborhood, you have wasted your money. On the other hand, if you buy a fixer upper in a good neighborhood and bring the place up to shape through some sweat equity, you've made a good investment. Also, don't buy the largest house in an area. Buy one of the smaller or mid sized houses, then the larger houses should help to raise the value of yours.

Another factor is quality of life. We live in a rural area that is zoned for animals. Several of our neighbors have horses, cows and chickens, which makes a good environment for children. However, we are only about thirty minutes from the city, so we have the culture and conveniences that a city offers within driving distance.

Another consideration is space. How much land do you want? For years, Keri and I lived in a small subdivision. After a while, the closeness of the neighbors became stifling. You may find that land is cheaper outside of the city, so you can purchase a house with more land for the same price that you could within the city.

Don't forget taxes (such an ugly word). Thankfully, there are still a few states left that don't charge an income tax:

Alaska	Florida
Nevada	New Hampshire
South Dakota	Tennessee
Texas	Washington
Wyoming	

If you live in a state that charges income tax, you may want to consider moving to one that doesn't. Look at it this way: Why should you send a certain percentage of your money to the state instead of putting it into your retirement account? However, make sure you investigate the total tax burden within a state such as sales tax and dividend and interest taxes that could offset the fact that the state has no income tax. Also, don't forget county taxes. The county that we live in has a much lower tax rate than the surrounding counties.

Don't Buy a Mansion

The first house we owned was a very small (approximately 850 square feet) two bedroom in a subdivision. Sometimes, in the early evening, I would sit in a lawn chair on the little patio behind the house and drink a beer while I cooked hamburgers or steaks. It was usually very peaceful and relaxing.

After living there for several years, some new neighbors moved in next door to us. Almost immediately, they installed an above ground pool in their backyard, right next to our patio. They were in the pool one evening while I was out there grilling. In addition to the noise (there must have been eight of them in the pool) it felt like they were only a few feet away from me (which I guess they were), looking right down on top of me. That was the straw that broke the camel's back. I had to get out of there.

Prior to this episode, Keri and I had already thought about moving. After we had our two daughters, the house that had once seemed cozy with just the two of us was really feeling small and cramped. Also, at that time, interest rates were very low (7 ½ percent, bear in mind this was nine years ago, before the incredibly low interest rates you can get now.). In addition, my commute to work was over an hour one way. However, there was one thing that little house definitely had going for it. Our payment was only $350 a month. I wish we still had a payment like that. But, we decided to bite the bullet and make the move.

We bought the house we currently live in nine years ago. The real estate market was very flat at the time and the house had been for sale almost a year. At one acre of land, we have the smallest lot on our street. Most of our neighbors have three or four acres, some have as many as twelve. The house itself has 1750 square feet, two bedrooms, a small office, and two bathrooms. We paid $85,000 for it. The present value is approximately $150,000.

Many of our friends have larger houses than we do and their children all have separate bedrooms. People seem surprised when they find out that our girls share a room. Occasionally, the girls complain about it too. Keri and I take a different view on this subject. We both remember a time when it was very common for siblings to share a room. I shared a room with my brother until he moved out to attend college. As hard as this is to believe, I don't think I suffered any long-term damage from it (perhaps my brother did, though...). There was an entire generation prior to this one who shared a bedroom with their brother or sister, so I'm not quite sure what changed that makes people think their kids will be deprived if they don't have a room of their own. Perhaps it's because a large percentage of people think their house is a reflection of themselves. And for many, perhaps it goes deeper than that. Part of their self worth is wrapped up with how big their house is. We are at the point now where we could potentially move up to a larger house, but we have decided that what we have is enough for us. That decision will save us thousands of dollars over the years we live here.

Don't Be Afraid to Buy Your House From the Owner

Most people that list through an agent have to allow for the agent's commission in the price of the house. That means you are paying part or all of the commission.

We bought our house from the original owners. They were an older couple who had built their dream house to their own specifications. They had a picture album that showed the house during all the different stages of construction. Seeing those pictures was the next best thing to actually being involved in the construction. There was also a file that contained all the paperwork on the appliances they had purchased, the well that was drilled, the water conditioner, etc. Because of this, we had a pretty good idea about the quality of the construction and all the appliances and fixtures they had purchased for the house.

In case you're thinking that we found our house in a couple of months, think again. We looked for over a year. I can't begin to tell you how many houses and areas we looked at before we purchased. However, remember that the time you spend looking is not lost time. We learned a lot about the type of house we wanted, the things we didn't want and about the area we eventually bought in. There is no substitute for actually driving around an area, up and down each street.

The way we approached our house search was to locate the general area we wanted to live in first. We narrowed it down to two areas, then focused on houses in those two neighborhoods. That way you know what you're getting into. We had spent so much time looking that by the time we bought we had a level of comfort about where we would be living.

Another factor to consider is how motivated is the seller? If the house has been on the market for a long time or there are conditions motivating the seller (divorce, job loss, etc.), it can work in your favor. As I mentioned before, the house we bought had been on the market for about a year. The couple was getting older and had gotten to the point where it was becoming a burden for them to maintain the house and yard. They knew they had to make a move into a home that required less maintenance. If you are hesitant about purchasing a house from someone who is motivated, remember that you aren't really taking advantage of them. In many cases you are actually doing them a favor because they have a need to sell. If there's no buyer, they can't fill their need, so in the long run, it's works out for both parties.

One other word of advice: Once you locate the house you want, unless you are a construction expert, go ahead and hire someone to inspect the house for structural soundness. It's well worth it for an investment that large.

Never Buy a New Car

Other than their house, probably the next biggest expense people have is their car payment. If you're thinking about buying a new car, I want you to do something before you pull the trigger. Go out into your back yard right now and dig a deep hole. Then, take several thousand dollars in cash, drop it in and cover it up. Better yet, put the money on your barbecue grill, soak it with some lighter fluid and put a match to it. Maybe if the money was packed tight enough you could at least grill some hot dogs over it. That's what you're doing when you buy a new car.

Lets' examine the positive aspects of buying a new car:

Status/Vanity

I can see it now: you glide into your driveway behind the wheel of your brand new vehicle. The new purchase sticker is conspicuously displayed on the side window for all to see. Of course you've made sure that you pick up the car on Saturday, so the neighbors will be outside doing yard work and perhaps will get the opportunity to witness your shiny new purchase. As you open the door, you anticipate the crush of your neighbors rushing over so they can drool over your shiny new car. With a feeling of sublime satisfaction, you bask in the glow of celebrity of the block status. However, after your 15 minutes of fame, you need to ask yourself: was it worth the several thousand dollars less that the car is worth now that it's officially a "used car" ?

Less money spent on maintenance/repairs

Yes, you should spend less money initially on maintenance and repairs with a new car. But you need to weigh that against the additional monthly outlay you will have on your car payment. An extra $150 to $200 every month adds up. Do you really think you will rack up $1,800 to $2,400 in car repair bills annually on your used car? Or put another way, assuming a four year car payment, do you think you will spend $7,200 to $9,600 fixing the used car? If you buy the right used car, you won't. I have driven used cars for years and have never exceeded that amount. I think the maximum I have ever spent on car repairs in one year was around $1,000. And I have never even come close to the four year total of $7,200.

Conversely, with the new car you *know* you will be spending the extra money each month, it's not a matter of guesswork. Whereas, if you buy a decent used car, you'll have some repairs, but not every month. There will be many months when there won't be any extra repairs. In order to be able to handle the months when you do get hit with a repair bill, set aside some money every month on a regular basis anyway (you would have spent it on the new car). If you don't have any major repair bills, you can just add that money to your retirement fund.

The new car smell (my wife's favorite reason)

This is one of those intangible factors that no doubt has a real pull for some people. However, it lasts about the length of time it takes your kid to get sick and puke in the back seat.

So, do you still think it makes more sense to buy a new car instead of a used one?

Used Cars

How to Buy a Used Car

You don't need to have the knowledge of a mechanic to find a good used car. The two most important qualities you need are patience and common sense. I spell out the common sense strategies in this section. Only you can supply the patience.

It is critical that you not be in a hurry when shopping for a used car. You have to be willing to do the necessary legwork required. If you feel like you can't devote the required time to this search, much as I hate to admit it, you might be better off purchasing a new car. Don't get me wrong though, purchasing a used car is still a much better financial decision than buying a new one, but only if you are willing to devote the time and effort to do it properly.

Before I get into the strategies you should use when locating a specific vehicle you want to purchase, let's consider how you should determine the make and model of the vehicle you want to buy. Keri and I always start from the point of what vehicles are both attractive and functional for our needs. Why buy a car that you think is ugly? I think you need to be happy with the type of car you drive, but it also needs to be functional. For us, the biggest factor for functionality is that it has to have 4 doors and be large enough to accommodate a family. Once you have a short list of vehicles, check the maintenance history on the make and model you like. Edmunds.com is a good resource for this. You want to select vehicles that have the best maintenance records, so hopefully you will have to spend less money on repairs over the years. Another thing to consider is gas mileage. If you purchase a gas-guzzler, you will pay for it over the years. Also, try to steer clear of a vehicle's first year of production, there are typically more mechanical problems with first year vehicles.

Check insurance rates before you buy. Target vehicles that are cheaper to insure. Your insurance company can provide you with this information over the phone before you buy.

Once you have narrowed your list down, you can begin your search for a specific vehicle. The classified ads and autotrader.com are where I usually start. I try to narrow the ads down to ones that mention excellent or mint condition. I have no interest in purchasing a car that was not immaculately maintained. You shouldn't either.

After you locate a few ads that look promising, prepare a short list of questions that you want to ask before you pick up the phone and call. The purpose of these questions is to save you valuable time. You will eliminate unnecessary trips if you ask the correct questions over the phone. Your goal is to try and eliminate the cars that won't meet your standards so you don't waste your time and money driving out to see a car that is a hunk of junk.

Checklist of what to ask on the phone:

Are you the original owner?

I prefer to buy used cars from the original owner. That helps eliminate some of the unknowns you might encounter. The exception to this is if there are full maintenance records from the previous owner. I own a conversion van that I bought from the second owner, however, there was a complete set of maintenance records that showed every single thing that was done to that van over the years. It tells a complete story. The most important piece of that story are the records that prove the oil was changed every 3,000 miles. With regard to maintenance history, oil change frequency is *absolutely critical*. In case you're wondering, the van now has over 150,000 miles on it and is still running great.

What is the mileage?

While low mileage is always desirable, there is a tradeoff involved with low mileage/high mileage. You are going to pay more for a low mileage vehicle than you will for one with high mileage. Conversely, you will be able to get the high mileage vehicle for less money. The reasoning being that there is less life remaining in a high mileage vehicle. While generally this is true, I think there are exceptions you should consider. If you ensure that you buy a vehicle with a reputation for lasting years and years with high mileage (like a Toyota) and you know that the vehicle has been properly maintained, don't necessarily let the mileage scare you away. However, make sure that the price is adjusted accordingly for the mileage. My Toyota had 95,000 miles and my van had over 120,000 miles when I purchased them. That being said, bear in mind that it is a little more risky to purchase a vehicle with high mileage. For me, the price difference is worth the risk. However, if you prefer to be on the safe side, stick with low mileage vehicles.

Has the car been in any accidents?

This is a critical question. I won't purchase a used car that has been involved in anything but the most minor fender bender. If you know or have any idea that the vehicle has been in an accident, walk away. There are too many unknowns. Such as: Is the frame bent? Does everything still seal like it should? Was it repaired properly? Is there any damage you can't see? I don't know about you, but I don't know enough about vehicles to determine the answers to those questions. So, your best bet is to play it safe. When in doubt, don't take the chance.

Has the car been regularly maintained and does the seller have records?

If there are no maintenance records, walk away. Don't take the owner's word, you want proof. Make it clear that you will want to review the records if you make the trip to see the car. I have encountered sellers who said they had records over the phone, but when I got there, the records could not be located.

Why are they selling the car?

This may seem like an obvious question, but the answers you get may be enlightening. The answer I like to hear is they are upgrading to a new vehicle. Some people just like to have a new vehicle every few years. There have been several times that I have asked this question and the person just started talking and kept going, eventually revealing information that told me I didn't want to investigate the car any farther, or was just so weird that my gut instinct told me to walk away.

If the vehicle does not pass any of these questions, you should be honest and thank the person for their time and end the call. If the vehicle passes the phone test, you need to arrange a time to meet and get directions to the owner's house. If the owner offers to meet you somewhere, politely decline saying that it's no problem at all to make the drive to their house.

You want to see their house.

Should I Buy a Used Car From this Person?

When you drive out to see the vehicle, you should ask yourself a question. Based on outward appearances, should I buy a used car from this *person*? That's right, you want to buy a car from a particular kind of person. When I actually meet them and see the car for the first time, I look for some signs that indicate a personality type. The kind of person you are looking for is someone who is anal-retentive (AR) to the max. You want someone who is obsessive about his or her possessions. Someone who worries about them, maintains them religiously, keeps them impeccably, unbearably clean. Someone who would never skip an oil change and would lose sleep over not being able to wash, wax, and detail the car every weekend. In other words, someone the exact opposite of myself. Personally, I would never buy a used car from me.

Here are the key indicators of the personality type you are looking for: How does this person's house look? Is it well maintained? Is the yard immaculate? Is the garage neat and tidy? If they score a no on these questions, you really need to think twice before you make an offer. If they don't maintain their house and other possessions just so, what makes you think they would maintain their car that way?

Here is a real life example of the perfect person to purchase a used car from. In 1998, I was in the market for a Toyota 4 Runner. I had looked at quite a few already. All of them were in less than immaculate shape. A few were OK, but nothing special. However, I was in no hurry (again, the cardinal rule of used car shopping, never be in a hurry, take your time). Eventually, my patience paid off.

Almost from the moment I pulled into the driveway, I knew I had found my man. The house looked like a model home. Every blade of grass in the lawn was standing at attention. His garage floor was so clean, you could have eaten off of it. An errant drop of oil had never touched that floor. The 4 Runner itself looked brand new. It looked so brand new that most of our friends thought we had bought a new one, when actually it was 7 years old (it's a 1991).

He proceeded to show me the car. When he lifted the hood, the engine was spotless. In the back of the vehicle, there was a tablecloth that he always kept there to keep any stains off the carpet. Then he reached into the glove compartment and pulled out the item that clenched the deal: The little black book.

In this little book, there was a record of all the maintenance that had ever been done to the vehicle. Complete with his comments on the quality of the work performed, the date, the place where the work was performed, mileage, and cost. As if that wasn't enough, in the front of the book was a section marked "GAS". The headings under this section were: Date, Cash or Credit, Station, Type, Gal, price, mileage. He recorded every single time the car was ever gassed, where it was gassed, the type of gas, the total price, and how many gallons were pumped !

I was speechless. Needless to say, this is the man you want to buy your used car from. Now, mind you, I never expect to find someone this perfect again, but this is an example of the personality type you are seeking.

Once you have located the car you think you want, there is one final thing you need to do. You need to arrange to have your mechanic give it the once over. If the mechanic detects any major problems, don't buy the vehicle. Any minor problems he encounters or potential upcoming problems can be negotiated when you make your offer.

The only concern I had about the 4 Runner was the mileage (95,000 miles). But since it had been so well maintained and it was a Toyota (I used to own a Toyota pickup that was still running at 205,000 miles when I sold it), I thought the risk was acceptable.

By the way, the 4 Runner is 11 years old now, over 180,000 miles, and still running.

Never Buy a Used Car From a Dealer

When you buy a used car from a dealer, what you are doing is paying the middleman, plain and simple. They received the car from a private party, marked up the price, and then they will sell it to you. I think there is perhaps a sense of security that some people get when they buy a used car from a dealer. Let's examine that notion to see if it's valid.

Does the dealer know the life history of that car like the original owner? Does he have an idea of whether or not the owner maintained the car properly? I'm sure that he will try to make some judgment about that, but does he have the time to devote to it that you do? Has he seen the owner's house and other possessions to give him some idea about how the owner takes care of his other possessions? Would he even care? The dealer has no intention of keeping the car long term (like you do). His objective is to buy it at the lowest price and move it off the car lot as soon as he can with the biggest profit he thinks he can get (that's his job).

Some people believe that if they encounter problems with the car, the dealer will "stand behind it". This is mostly a false sense of security. I'm sure that whatever the length of the warranty is, it is limited, then beyond that time, you're on your own (assuming they fix any problems during the warranty period correctly and in a timely fashion).

Unfortunately there are unscrupulous dealers out there. There's no telling how many problems can be hidden with a good car detailing and wax job. Personally, I have never bought a used car from a dealer and never will.

Drive it Till the Wheels Fall Off

There is no doubt that Americans have a love affair with their cars. As soon as they get one paid off, they start shopping for a new one. They want to have the "Latest Model". Many Americans swap cars every three or   four years.

Here's a novel idea: keep your car as long as you can. Once you have it paid off, that's like money in the bank every month. However, this may require you to change your mindset. You need to stop viewing your car as a status symbol and see it for what it really is (or should be), a form of transportation, a means of getting from one place to another.

Assuming a car payment of $150 a month, you can save $1,800 a year for every year you drive your paid off vehicle.

Here's another way to look at it: Let's assume you get a new car every five years. If you kept that car five years longer (a total of ten years) and it was paid off during those last five years, how much money would you save in a lifetime? $1,800 per year times 5 = $9000 dollars. Now, lets use the timespan from when you are age 20 to age 75. That would add up to 25 years with no car payment. 25 years times $1,800 = $45,000. In reality, the amount of money would be quite a lot more than that if you include the interest you could have earned on the money.

So, is that feeling of status from driving a new car worth the thousands of dollars it will cost you over your lifetime?

Estate Auction

Why Buy it New When You Can Buy it Used?

As with purchasing a car or house, why should you buy anything new when in many cases, you can buy the same thing used at less than half the price?

In the twenty years Keri and I have been married, there have only been a handful of times we bought a new piece of furniture. After we first got married, we purchased a beautiful Ethan Allen dining room set used from a private person. If memory serves me right, we paid $200 for it. We also bought our china cabinet used for $75 at an Estate sale many years ago. The king-size bed we have is used, we traded our old personal computer to a couple who had just purchased a waterbed. The Steelcase desk in Keri's office was purchased used at a furniture outlet. It's as sturdy as a battleship.

I think our favorite story is the antique dresser and mirror we bought many years ago from an older couple. After we saw it for the first time, we told the couple that we liked it, but it was the first one we had looked at, and we wanted to check out a few others. When we left, we told them we might be back. As it turns out, that first one was the one we liked most. When we returned, without any prompting from us, the old couple told us they had discussed it while we were gone and had decided if we returned they would reduce the price $10 because we were such a nice young couple.

Even when we have bought items like appliances new, we try to purchase scratch and dent items. Our washing machine is a top of the line Maytag that had a fairly large scratch on the front. We got it for about half the normal price. After we brought it home, I spray painted the scratch with almond paint, and now you can hardly tell the difference. We have also purchased a scratch and dent dryer and dishwasher. The dryer had a small dent on the side and one of the legs on the dishwasher was a little bent. Both were purchased at a large discount from the new price.

Consider shopping on line at amazon.com and half.com. I have bought video games, books, and even a toaster oven on line. Many of these items can be purchased for less than half their normal price. Another bonus of on line shopping is no tax. However, you need to be sensitive to shipping costs. But even considering shipping, most of the items are less expensive. You also have to factor in that it takes less time to shop on line, less hassle, less wear and tear on your vehicle, and less gas.

Here's the cardinal rule for buying anything used. Never pay the asking price. *Always* make an offer. You have nothing to lose by making an offer.

Here is a list of some of the things that we have bought used:

Cars
Houses

Couches
Dining room table and chairs
China Cabinet
Chairs
VCR
Clothes
Books
Televisions
Cookware
Computer Equipment
Videogame system and game cartridges
Lawnmowers
Exercise Equipment
Piano
Washing machine
Dryer
Pop up camper
Toaster Oven
Desk

Car and House Insurance

Get those insurance policies out and review them.

Car Insurance

Before you buy a vehicle, call your insurance company to find out how much it will cost to insure. Stay away from high insurance premium vehicles.

If your collision deductible is less than $1,000, consider bumping it up, it will save you money every month. Also consider raising the deductible on your comprehensive to $500. In addition, if your car is worth less than $3,000 or $4,000, consider dropping the collision altogether.

Homeowners Insurance

Raise your deductibles to $1,000.

One word of caution, raising these deductibles is based on the law of averages, you need to consider the possibility that you might have a claim and have to pay more out of pocket expense than before. However, if you aren't "claim happy" and are a safe driver, in the long run, you should save money.

Get Out of the Restaurants and Back in the Kitchen

Without a doubt, this is the most difficult strategy for us to stick with, but it's also where we spend a lot of our money. There are so many times at the end of the day when neither Keri nor I feel like preparing something for dinner, so we wind up going out somewhere or getting take out food. The other problem is we both like going out to eat.

However, we are eating out less than we used to, and when we cook at home, we try to make inexpensive meals. Here are some of the strategies we use to reduce our cooking bills:

We try to prepare meals that can be eaten more than once. Once or twice a month, Keri makes soup that we can get three meals out of.

We eat less red meat and more chicken instead. Not only is it healthier, it's cheaper. We try not to buy chicken unless it's on sale. We usually buy about 10 pounds and split it up into separate freezer bags. We have an extra refrigerator out in our garage (it was given to us by some friends who got a new one, they just wanted someone to take it away).

Since I now telecommute, it's more convenient for me to cook. At four o'clock, I can put some chicken in the oven, then go right back to work.

When we do go to restaurants, we try to hit them on nights when kids eat free. Some of the restaurants also offer coupons in the Sunday papers. We use those whenever we can. Another money saver is to split a meal. In case you haven't noticed, at many restaurants, the portions are huge. Quite often, when Keri and I go out, we get one entree for both of us.

It's something we still fight on a day to day basis, but we are definitely eating out less than we used to.

ebt, Over 40, With No Retirement Savings HELP!

Coupons? Are You Out of Your Mind? 97

section of the garage devoted to non perishable
s like paper towels, laundry detergent, bleach,
ed goods, etc. There are two advantages to buying
he price is cheaper and it also allows you to wait
eally find a good price before you buy. When you
n smaller quantities, you sometimes run out and
to buy something when it's not on sale.

Coupons? Are You Out of Your Mind?

I get the biggest kick out of watching our friends' faces when Keri tells them that I clip coupons. I even have a blue organizer that she bought for me to keep them in. Every Sunday morning when I get the newspaper, the first thing I do is clip out the coupons.

I also need to make a public statement here. For years, I used to kid my wife about using coupons, making fun of her using them (or so *she* says, I don't quite remember it that way…) but anyway, assuming she's correct, here's my public apology:

"I was wrong about coupons, Keri knew all along that it was a good strategy, please accept my humble apologies". Now that that's out of the way:

If it helps, maybe you should think about coupons this way.

COUPONS = MONEY.   I think about my coupon organizer as being a wallet full of money.

If I go to the grocery store and save $5 using coupons, that's $5 that did not come out of my checking account. Now what's the real difference between a coupon and money?

These are the strategies that I have found useful when using them: Only clip coupons for items you would normally use (or more accurately, only clip coupons for the stuff your wife really likes) If you try to substitute an "inferior product" thinking she won't notice, guess again. Believe me, it's just not worth the hassle. The exception to this rule is that some folks belong to "coupon clubs". They get together and swap coupons, as in: "I'll trade you one Tide coupon for the Downy fabric softener coupon." Sorry, but I can't see myself doing that just yet, but for the folks that do, I'm sure it pays off.

Try to combine your coupons with an item that's on sale. That way, you get the maximum discount.

Did you know that if you call a company and give them feedback on their products, they will send you coupons? Just about every item you buy has an 800 number for you to call. I have gotten coupons for dog food, coffee creamer, detergent, etc.

We have a
staple iten
pasta, canr
in bulk. T
until you
purchase
are forced

Buy

With non-perishable items,
the grocery store I go to had
toilet paper. In addition, right
of those red ticket dispens
coupons were for fifty cents o
of toilet paper. My final price
coupon was $1 per four pack. I

Also, bear in mind that just bec
display says "Limit two per cus
mean they won't sell you more.
store limits many times, and t
challenged. It just takes a little ch
in life). The worst they can do i
You have nothing to lose and ever
total of fifty packages. Just in co
savings. Who says coupons don't
disadvantage is that now our garage
warehouse. The upside is now we ne

Teenagers
(How to get them out of the
house without bankrupting you)

Our daughters, Mary (the oldest) and Kathleen (the youngest), are the greatest thing that ever happened to Keri and me. I'm amazed at how beautiful and intelligent they are. However, having kids is an expensive proposition, no matter how you look at it. During the span of one five minute conversation, my oldest daughter asked for her own private phone line, satellite TV, and caller ID. Accordingly, your ability to say no will determine whether or not you will be in the poor house.

Keri and I have been striving to introduce our girls to the *beauty* of buying things used. Occasionally, I take them to Barnes & Noble or Borders on the weekend. We used to walk out with an armload of books and $50 poorer. Now, I give them each a pad and pencil and let them write down the title and author of the books they like. Then we go home and order them used off of half.com or abebooks.com. To offset the disappointment of not buying the books at the retail store, there is a little excitement and anticipation involved with receiving a book in the mail.

When my youngest daughter wanted a Nintendo, we bought the system and the games used on Half.com.

Lest you think we never spend any money on our kids, let me tell you about where we do spend money on them. We have some fairly large regular expenses that we think will pay off in the future.

We initially enrolled our oldest daughter into public Kindergarten. During that year, I was on the School Advisory Council for parents. The school district was in the midst of introducing an entirely new curriculum and approach to schooling called "Blueprint 2000". It included such brilliant concepts as "Inventive spelling". I learned enough about the curriculum to determine that they were in essence performing an experiment with our child's education. When I questioned the administration about some of the methods they were using, I was told somewhat condescendingly that the methods that had been used to teach us when we were kids were outdated and didn't really work in today's world. Before the end of the school year, we were determined to find another school for our child.

Keri did a fair amount of research in an effort to determine what schools would offer the best education. She spoke with a person who worked for the state board of education. Amazingly, the person was actually honest enough to admit that the Catholic Schools provide an excellent education.

Both our daughters have been in Catholic School for several years now and we are very pleased with the education they are receiving. But it's an expenditure we had never really anticipated. We had both assumed that our children would go to public school.

Both of us went to public school and felt that we received a pretty good education, but the reality is today's schools are not the same as when we were kids. If you have school age children, or children that are almost school age, you owe it to yourself to find out as much as you can about your local school. Hopefully, you won't be as surprised and disappointed as we were.

As you can probably tell, the importance of a good education is stressed in our house. In addition to providing our daughters with a good foundation for the future, there is a potential financial advantage. We are hoping that they will receive scholarships that will help defray the cost of a college education.

Another expenditure we have is music lessons. We have offered to both of our daughters that we would buy any instrument that they were interested in and provide them with lessons. Our youngest daughter has been taking piano lessons for a couple of years now. However, instead of rushing out and buying a brand new piano, we bought a used one for $675 dollars. Just recently, our oldest daughter expressed an interest in learning the guitar. Once again, instead of buying a new one, we bought one used.

Want a good strategy for helping reduce all those huge after Christmas bills? Have you ever considered buying used Christmas presents (Gasp!) for your kids? Just this past Christmas, along with the new gifts they received, they got a used book and some used computer games on Christmas morning.

We have also been trying to teach our daughters the value of saving. We took all the loose change from the change drawer and used it to open savings accounts for then. Once the accounts were open, I offered to match any money they deposited with the following conditions: They can't withdraw the money and the offer is subject to change or cancellation at my discretion. If they don't receive any college scholarships, the money they have accumulated could be applied towards their college tuition.

The other day, I had to shell out $50 to match the money my youngest daughter deposited. This might be working so well, we'll wind up in the poor house.

Telecommute

If you have the option to telecommute available to you, consider taking it. Unfortunately, few employers allow employees to telecommute. If yours does, you should think twice if you have not taken advantage of the option.

My employer has a very forward thinking telecommuting policy. However, even in a company that has a progressive policy, you can encounter managers who are reluctant to actually implement the policy. Before you jump right in, you need to try and get a feel about whether or not your manager really supports the idea, or just gives it lip service.

Unfortunately, some managers have an "Old School" mentality. They want to see you sitting at your desk. They want to "see you sweat". Also, some are concerned that employees will take advantage of the situation. While there is some truth to that, what's probably more accurate is some employees will take advantage of any situation, it doesn't matter whether they are telecommuting or not. Accordingly, good employees will work hard wherever they are.

I now work longer hours than I did before because I don't have to waste time commuting. I also check my emails on the weekend and in the evenings. In addition, I'm more devoted to my job because I like telecommuting so much.

What's kind of funny is that I was slow to take advantage of the policy. It was one of those things where I kept telling myself "I really need to try that", but just never got around to it. What finally turned things around for me is that I had to have an operation. During the recovery period, I was able to return to work earlier and easier because I was able to telecommute. After doing it for a couple of weeks, I discovered that I really liked it and that it worked for me.

There are several advantages to telecommuting for both the employer and the employee. The employer saves on office space, which converts to real dollar savings for a company. In addition, in many cases, employees are able to put in more hours because the commute time has been eliminated. Another intangible but no less important benefit for an employer is a more dedicated work force.

For myself, I think not having that daily drive, not sitting in traffic, breathing exhaust fumes is the greatest benefit to me. The monetary benefits are also pretty substantial: less money spent on gas, I also don't have to spend money having to buy all those office "Go to work clothes". It also makes it easier to eat leftovers at home instead of going out for lunch. In addition, I was able to lower my car insurance because I drive a lot fewer miles each year, I don't have as much wear and tear on my vehicle, and I spend less money on repairs.

Exercise

What does exercise have to do with retirement, financial security, and saving money?

If your goal is to retire one day, do you want to be overweight and out of shape? Do you want to be burdened with chronic diseases that limit your ability to enjoy life and pursue the activities you want? What good is retirement if you are physically limited in the things you can do? It makes sense to me that at whatever age you retire, you want to be in good physical condition.

Another benefit of exercise is that it's an excellent stress reliever. I work out with weights on a regular basis. Usually two or three times a week. The difference is very noticeable to me. If I get lazy and go for a while without working out, I feel lethargic. I get irritable and grumpy. Weight training also helps you maintain muscle mass and bone density. These two areas are critical when people get older. One of the reasons people get so feeble when they get old is that they don't have much muscle left. Weight training can help slow the aging process.

I also walk on a regular basis. If you aren't doing any type of cardiovascular exercise you should start walking, riding a bike, swimming, dancing, etc.

There is also a potential financial benefit to maintaining your health. One of the major expenses an older person can face is prescription drug costs. If you are relatively healthy, you may not need to spend as much money on prescription drugs.

PART THREE

Saving For Retirement

Just Do it (Join the 401K)

If you have a tax deferred savings plan at work, just join it. For most employees, it's the 401K, for employees of non-profit organizations, it's the 403(b). This is the first place you should look when you start saving. The money you put into your 401K is tax deductible. You pay no taxes on the money going into the account, however, when you retire and begin to withdraw, then the money is taxed.

Don't get paralyzed by the thought of which mutual fund within the 401K you want to put your money into. If you're ultra conservative, put your money into a stable value fund. If you're a little less conservative, you can put 60 to 70 percent in a bond fund, and the other percentage in a stock fund. If you're an aggressive investor, you can put most of your money into the stock funds. The traditional wisdom is the younger you are, the more time you have to recover any losses that could be incurred in a shorter time frame, so you can be more aggressive with your money. I won't attempt to address all the different asset allocation strategies you should use. You can consult with a reputable financial advisor about that. The point I want to make is that it's better to do something than nothing. If you do nothing, come retirement time, that's exactly what you'll have.

Another advantage of the 401K is that it's automatically deducted from your paycheck on a regular basis. The money never touches your bank account. For many people, that's the only way they can save, out of sight, out of mind.

Many companies offer a match for the 401K. For example, my company matches fifty percent up to six percent of employee contribution. So, if I contribute six percent, the company kicks in three percent. You can't beat that. So, at a minimum, you should try to contribute at least to the level your company matches.

However, don't make the mistake of investing a huge portion of your money in your own company's stock. If your company encounters hard times and their stock price drops, your exposure could be huge. Also, if you got laid off at the same time the stock price dropped, it would be a double whammy. With that in mind, if the company offers it's stock at a discount to employees, you need to consider allocating some of your money to it, but make sure it's only a portion of your money.

Roth IRA

Once you have contributed the maximum amount your employer matches in your tax-deferred account, you want to consider opening a Roth IRA. It is named after former Senator William V. Roth, Jr. (thanks Mr. Roth).

The money you put into a Roth is after tax money. However, there are some advantages of a Roth IRA over a traditional IRA:

You don't have to automatically take distributions from a Roth at age 70 ½. If you have enough money, you don't have to use the money in your Roth. Also, once the money is in the account, it's non taxable. It's growth will be non taxable, and when you withdraw the money, it's non taxable. For me, that option is awfully attractive. I really like the idea of having non-taxable money at retirement time.

Don't Give up Responsibility For Your Money

In this entire world, who is your money more important to than you? Who can you trust with your money more than you?

There's nothing wrong with seeking financial advice or having a financial advisor manage your money if that's what you want to do, but don't ever make the mistake of turning your hard earned cash over to someone else and never giving it another thought. If you do, be prepared to suffer the consequences. You should always be aware of the potential risks associated with an investment as well as the potential gains.

There is no better example of this than the stock market crash of the last couple of years. Sadly, there are people who lost all or a large portion of their savings because they entrusted their money to someone else to manage and were not aware of the potential risks they were facing.

Become educated on the types of investments your financial advisor wants to place your money into. If you don't understand the investment, read up on it. Don't take the lazy way out. You could wind up paying for it dearly.

Have some idea of what your long-term objectives are. Will you be happy with a small return on your investment, knowing that your principal is fairly secure? Are you looking for a larger potential return and are you willing to be a little more risky with your money? What is your time frame for when you will need the money you want to invest? If your time frame is fairly short (less than five years), you probably don't want your money in the stock market. If you are investing long term, you want to consider placing some of your money in stocks. A lot of it comes down to your tolerance for pain. If you can't stand to watch your account balance go down for any extended period of time, you probably don't want to have a lot of your money invested in stocks.

One thing you should always ask a financial advisor: "What is the worst case scenario with this investment?" Also, make sure that you're always aware of any changes your financial advisor makes to your portfolio.

Build a Cushion

Our cash cushion helped us make it through this past year without piling up credit card debt. We actually had to dip into it quite a bit, so we are now in the process of trying to rebuild it. One of the reasons that Keri and I got into so much debt in the past was because we didn't have a cash cushion. Most of our lives we have lived from paycheck to paycheck.

When you have no cushion, the unexpected medical bill or car repair might force you to use your credit card. When you use it, you have the intent to pay it off as soon as possible, but all too often another unexpected bill comes along and you have to use the credit card for that too. Before you know it, you've piled up more credit card debt.

As with paying down your debts, one way to fund your cushion is to take any monetary gifts you receive like that check from your Mom at Christmas or on your birthday and save it instead of spending it. If you receive any bonuses at work, save them. The income tax refund? Save it.

I receive an annual bonus in March. We are going to use it to rebuild our cushion. In addition to funding the cushion with lump sums like these, you should also set aside a certain amount each month or each time you get paid.

Compound Interest

Compound interest is a wonderful thing. You need to understand this concept. It will help emphasize the importance of saving.

If you save $1,000 at 5 percent interest, in a year you'll have $1,050. The next year, you'll be earning interest on $1,050, not $1,000. That's why compound interest is so powerful.

There is a well known rule called the rule of 72. You can use it to compute how long it would take an amount of money to double at a particular rate of interest.

For example, if the interest rate is 5 percent, to calculate the amount of time it would take to double your money, simply divide 72 by the interest rate. 72 / 5 = 14.4 years. In 14.4 years, your money would double. Conversely, if you want to know what interest rate your money would have to earn in order to double your money in a given time frame, just divide the number of years into 72. 72 / 8 years = 9. So, if you earn 9 percent interest, your money will double in 8 years.

At one point I attempted to explain the concept of compound interest to my daughters so they could understand the power of saving. What is interesting is that at some point before their eyes glazed over, I think they actually began to grasp the idea.

PART FOUR

Keeping Your Mind Right

Total Denial Could Equal Total Disaster

Don't make the mistake of denying yourself everything. It's too easy to build up a resentment that could create a backlash. Every once in a while, go out to dinner in a nice restaurant. Periodically, take the weekend off and go to a hotel.

I have no desire to never again be able to go out to a fine restaurant and have a good steak dinner with a nice bottle of wine. The up side is that you will enjoy the occasional dinner out more than you did when you were going out to eat all the time. It will become a special occasion again.

Keri and I also enjoy going away on the weekend every now and then. Life would be pretty boring if you never did anything like that.

Think For Yourself

We have become a super sized society. Super sized houses, super sized meals, super sized debts, super sized wants and super sized needs. Your ability to think for yourself and go against the grain is the most powerful tool you have against the onslaught of all this super sized brainwashing.

I am the type of person who has always thought outside of the box, so for me, it hasn't been too difficult to go against the societal norms of wanting the bigger house, the keeping up with the Jones mentality.

I attribute much of this attitude to my upbringing. My Father taught me to always question what people told me and the things I read. He did not accept things at face value, he always looked under the surface to see what the real meaning and value of something was. He believed that everyone has their own agenda and in many cases, they might be trying to sell you something. I can't think of any better or truer advice.

What about you? Are you the type of person who can go against the grain or are you going to unthinkingly accept what has become the modern American ideal of bigger houses, bigger cars, bigger debts?

Is your car a status symbol to you or just a mode of transportation? Do you need to wear a designer label on your clothes to feel good about yourself, or do you just want to wear decent, functional clothing? Are you ashamed to buy used furniture, or would you feel good about getting a great deal on an older, well-made piece of furniture? Do you need to satisfy the urge to purchase something right now or will you have the patience and maturity to wait until you have saved up enough money to pay cash for it? Do you need to live in a mansion that you can show off to all your friends, or will you be happy in a house that's just big enough to suit your needs?

The answer to these questions will determine to a great extent how much money you will be able to accumulate for retirement.

A lot of this amounts to being conscious of what you are doing with your life. Are you going to blindly spend your way through life, or do you have the presence of mind to sit down and choose your priorities wisely. It takes a certain amount of strength and courage of conviction to be a little bit different than everyone else.

Don't Quit

One of the hardest things to deal with is when you suffer some kind of setback as you're working toward your goals of paying down debt and accumulating savings. When I started paying down our debts, I would usually have some short-term goal in mind like paying the Sears card off in two months or paying the dentist bill in three months. Then an unexpected expense would come along and I would have to deal with that, not allowing me to reach my goals as soon as I wanted.

Invariably, setbacks occur. The key is to not let those types of setbacks discourage you. They are normal and happen to everyone. Remember that you're in this for the long term.

Remember that you will have fits and starts. At times you will be more motivated than others. Just remember that it's normal and all part of the process.

A couple of years into it, you will have a better perspective. You will begin to realize just how much you have accomplished. So remember, you're in this for the long haul, not for just a year or two.

Appendix

The Shopping Decision Tree

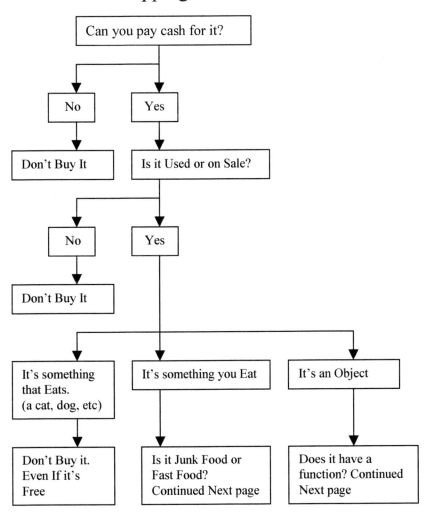

Can you pay cash for it?

No → Don't Buy It

Yes → Is it Used or on Sale?

No → Don't Buy It

Yes →

It's something that Eats. (a cat, dog, etc) → Don't Buy it. Even If it's Free

It's something you Eat → Is it Junk Food or Fast Food? Continued Next page

It's an Object → Does it have a function? Continued Next page

Appendix

The Shopping Decision Tree (continued)

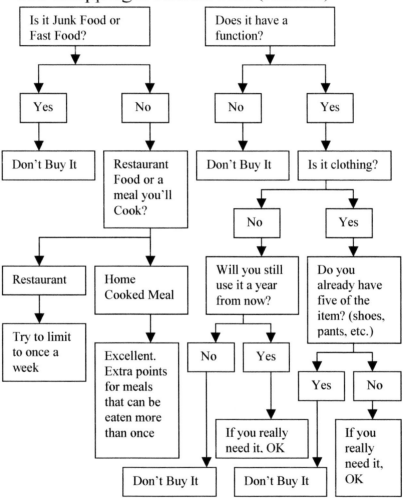

Resources

Here is a list of resources that have provided inspiration and insight to me in my journey toward financial stability. The books listed are notable exceptions to the "financial books are boring" rule.

Books:

Your Money or Your Life: Transforming Your Relationship with Money and Achieving Financial Independence

Authors: Joe Dominguez and Vicki Robin
Publisher: Penguin
ISBN: 0-14-028678-0

This is the type of book about which people say: "It changed my life". After you read it you may never view work or money the same way again. A truly wonderful book.

Cashing in on the American Dream: How to Retire at 35

Author: Paul Terhorst
Publisher: Bantam Books
ISBN: 0-553-27815-0

Tired of life on the corporate treadmill, Paul Terhorst retired from his Accounting career at age 35. This book is a classic on early retirement. By tapping into equity that you may already have (like your house), and keeping your expenses at a reasonable level, you may find out that you are closer to retirement than you think. It is currently out of print, but you can still find used copies on the Internet. An excellent book, highly readable

The Millionaire Next Door

Authors: Thomas J. Stanley, Ph.D.
          William D. Danko, Ph.D.
Publisher: Longstreet Press
ISBN: 1-56352-330-2

This book dispels the myth that most millionaires live an ostentatious lifestyle. Quite to the contrary. They became millionaires by living within their means. The book also drives home the point that wealth is not what you make, it's what you keep. Highly Recommended.

The Richest Man in Babylon

Author: George S. Clason
Publisher: Signet
ISBN: 0-451-20536-7

An investment classic originally published in 1926. Investment concepts told as "Babylonian parables". This book delivers a simple, yet powerful message.

Retire Early – And Live the Life You Want Now

Author: John F. Wasik
Publisher: Owl Books
ISBN: 0-8050-6349-8

I like this book because it covers both the financial and emotional aspects of planning for a successful early retirement. Highly recommended.

Last Minute Retirement Planning

Author: Steven M. Rosenberg, CFP
Publisher: Career Press
ISBN: 1-56414-376-7

This book contains down to earth, realistic advice. It addresses the reality of having to make choices with your money and the necessity of focusing on your priorities.

How to Retire Early and Live Well (With Less than a million dollars)

Author: Gillette Edmunds
Publisher: Adams Media Corporation
ISBN: 1-58062-201-1

The thing I like about this book is that there are parts devoted to the emotional issues associated with retirement such as how you will handle years when the value of your investment portfolio decreases.

The Average Family's Guide To Financial Freedom

Authors: Bill and Mary Toohey
Publisher: John Wiley & Sons, Inc.
ISBN: 0-451-20536-7

This book has a tremendous amount of credibility because Bill and Mary Toohey are not professional financial consultants, they are average people who accumulated an impressive sum of money on modest incomes.

The Wealthy Barber

Author: David Chilton
Publisher: Prima Publishing
ISBN: 0-761-51311-6

Sound financial advice written with a very approachable style.

Internet:

The Retire Early Website - retireearlyhomepage.com

This web site was created by John P. Greaney. Before he retired at age 38, Mr. Greaney was an engineer. I truly enjoyed finding this site because of the irreverent, "tell it like it is" style that is employed.

The Simple Living Website - Simpleliving.net

Provides Tools, Examples & Contacts for Conscious, Simple Living. There is a forums section on this site with email conversations regarding a variety of simple living topics.

The Dollar Stretcher - Stretcher.com

A truckload of ideas for how to save money.

Abebooks - Abebooks.com

An excellent resource to locate used, rare, and out of print books.

Half.com

Various items available at discounted prices.

Autotrader.com

An good resource for locating used cars

Index

Air conditioning, 60
Asset allocation, 111
Appliances, 69, 90
   scratch and dent, 90

Bonds, 111
Budget, 55
Buying in bulk, 99

Cable TV, 60
Cars
   Accidents, 78
   first year vehicles, 76
   gas mileage, 76
   how to buy used, 75
   insurance rates,76, 93,106
   keeping after paid off, 87
   maintenance, 72, 76-78
   mechanical inspection, 83
   mileage, 77
   new cars, 71
   status, 71, 72, 87, 126
   used cars, 72, 75, 77, 81,
        85, 135
   used car dealers, 85
   who to buy from, 81
Cash cushion, 117
   Why, 117
   how to build one, 117
Christmas presents, 103

Clothes, 43, 57, 91, 106, 126
   Status clothes, 126
   work clothes, 106
Collecting, 47
Compound interest, 119
Conscious living, 126, 134
Cooking, 95
Coupons, 51, 96-98
   how to get them, 98
   strategies, 98
Corporate world, 19
Credit cards, 15, 20, 39, 40,
       49, 50, 117
Debt
   getting out of, 39, 40
Denial
   danger of denial, 123

Electricity
   how to save, 60
Exercise, 107, 108

Furniture
   new, 89
   used, 126

Global Economy, 25
Home equity loan, 40
Houses
   Emotional issues, 66

Inspection, 70
Interest rates, 59
Location, 63, 70
Refinancing, 59
building houses, 63
buying from owner, 69
taxes, 64

Interest
Compound, 119
Earned, 88
On loans, 39, 40, 44
Rates, 59, 66
Insurance
Car, 76, 93, 106
Deductibles, 93, 94
House, 93

Job market, 25
Junk, 43-45

Kids
sharing a room, 66

Light bulbs
compact fluorescent, 61

Magazine
Subscriptions, 61
Mistakes
putting behind you, 27,28
Money
real money, 49

Pensions
cash Balance, 34, 35
traditional, 34
Possessions, 37, 43, 51,81,85

Raises, 20, 21
Responsibility
for your money, 115
Restaurants, 95, 96
how to spend less, 96
Retirement Age
will you be there, 33
Roth IRA, 34, 113
Rule of 72, 119

Salary, 19-22, 28, 34
Satellite TV, 60, 101
Setbacks
how to deal with, 127
Schools
Public, 102, 103
Private, 56, 102
Social Security, 30, 34, 35
will it be there, 34
will you be there, 33
Spouse
Communication with, 51
State Tax, 64
Status symbols
Cars, 71, 72, 87,
88, 126
houses, 126
Storage units, 44
Subscriptions
Magazines, 61
Newspaper, 61

Taxes
county, 64
property, 57, 64
refund, 117
sales, 90
state tax, 64

Tax deferred plans
    401K, 111, 112
    403(b), 111, 112
Teenagers, 101
    Saving, 104
    Wants, 101
Telecommuting, 23, 96, 105
    company advantage, 106
    employee advantage, 106
    management attitude, 105
Time
    and life, 29-31
    value of, 37-39, 44
Television
    Cable, 60
    Satellite, 60, 101

Value
    what do you value, 37

Water heater
    changing elements, 60, 61
    timer, 60
Windfalls
    what to do with them, 40
Work
    why do you do it?, 29-31

Order Form

Fax Orders: 813-907-2652. Send this form.

Toll Free Telephone Orders: 866-362-0599 Have your credit card handy.

Email Orders: everlovebohannon@aol.com

Postal Orders: Everlove and Bohannon Publishing, PO Box 7411 Wesley Chapel FL   33544-0107

I want ____ copies of **I'm in Debt, Over 40, With No Retirement Savings HELP!** For $14.95 each.

Name:_____

Address:_____

City/State/Zip:_____

Telephone:_____

Email:_____

Sales Tax: Please add 6% for books shipped to Florida addresses.

Shipping: $4.00 for the first book and $2.00 for each additional book.

My check or money order for $_____ is enclosed.
Please charge my:
__ Visa __ MasterCard __ American Express

Card Number:_____

Name on card:_____ Exp. Date:_____